D1142658

My First Missal

my name is

I was born on

I was baptized on

I made my First Communion on

This book was given to me by

Pauline
BOOKS & MEDIA

Nihil Obstat, Mgr Dennis F Sheehan, SJD
Imprimatur, May 11, 1994

Illustrations:
    Carla Cortesi
    Compiled by Maria Luisa Benigni

Translation:
    Edmund C. Lane, SSP

Original title: Il Mio Primo Messalino
© 1990, Paoline Editoriale Libri
Via Francesco Albani, 21-20149 Milan, Italy

English Edition
© Pauline Books & Media UK, 2004

ISBN 1-904 785-02-6

Published in the United Kingdom by
Pauline Books & Media
Middle Green
Slough SL3 6BS
www.pauline-uk.org

Stampa: www.AGAM.it

Contents

It's Sunday!

Let's rejoice because **God** the **Father**
　　　has made everything that is.

Let's rejoice because **Jesus Christ**
　　　has risen from the dead.

Let's rejoice because the **Holy Spirit**
　　　makes us one in love.

In the name of the **Father**, and of the **Son**,
　　　and of the **Holy Spirit**,
　　　　together, young and old,
　　　　　let us celebrate the **Eucharist**.

**This is the day
the Lord has made!**

We celebrate
the eucharist

Come

Introductory Rites

Entrance song

While the priest comes in, we sing a song that shows how happy we are to be able to be part of this celebration.

The priest greets us

PRIEST: In the name of the Father, and of the Son, and of the Holy Spirit.

PEOPLE: **Amen.**

PRIEST: The Lord be with you.

PEOPLE: **And also with you.**

Penitential Rite

We ask for forgiveness

PRIEST: My brothers and sisters, to prepare
ourselves to celebrate the sacred
mysteries, let us call to mind our sins.

*After thinking about what wrong things we have
done, we all say together:*

PEOPLE: **I confess to almighty God,**
and to you,
my brothers and sisters,
that I have sinned
through my own fault
in my thoughts
and in my words,
in what I have done,
and in what I have failed to do;
and I ask blessed Mary, ever virgin,
all the angels and saints,
and you,
my brothers and sisters,
to pray for me
to the Lord our God.

Sometimes we might say another prayer instead.

PRIEST: May almighty God have mercy on us,
forgive us our sins,
and bring us to everlasting life.

PEOPLE: **Amen.**

13

Invocations

PRIEST: Lord, have mercy.

PEOPLE: **Lord, have mercy.**

PRIEST: Christ, have mercy.

PEOPLE: **Christ, have mercy.**

PRIEST: Lord, have mercy.

PEOPLE: **Lord, have mercy.**

GLORIA
We praise and give thanks to God

This is a song that praises God. It is said or sung on feast days and on all Sundays except during Lent and Advent.

PEOPLE:
Glory to God in the highest,
and peace to his people on earth.

Lord God, heavenly King,
almighty God and Father,
we worship you,
we give you thanks,
we praise you for your glory.

Lord Jesus Christ,
only Son of the Father,
Lord God, Lamb of God,
you take away the sin of the world:
have mercy on us;
you are seated
at the right hand of the Father:
receive our prayer.

For you alone are the Holy One,
you alone are the Lord,
you alone are the Most High,
Jesus Christ,
with the Holy Spirit,
in the glory of God the Father.
Amen.

After this hymn, the priest says a prayer that tells us what today's celebration is about. At the end of the prayer, we answer:

PEOPLE: **Amen.**

Listen

The Liturgy of the Word

When we love someone, we enjoy listening to what that person has to say. The Bible tells us what God has done for our human family since time began. This is why we want to listen to the readings. It is God speaking to us today.

The first **reading**

Most of the time this reading is taken from the Old Testament, that part of the Bible that tells us what God did and said before the coming of Jesus.

The reader ends by saying:

This is the word of the Lord.

We answer:

PEOPLE: **Thanks be to God.**

The second reading

This reading is taken from the letters that the Apostles wrote to the very first Christians, and so also to us.

The reader ends by saying:

> This is the word of the Lord.

We answer:

PEOPLE: **Thanks be to God.**

The Gospel

We stand up to sing the Alleluia and to get ready to listen to the Gospel.

DEACON (OR PRIEST): The Lord be with you.

PEOPLE: **And also with you.**

DEACON (OR PRIEST): A reading from the holy Gospel according to *(one of the four evangelists).*

PEOPLE: **Glory to you, Lord.**

After reading the Gospel,
the deacon (or priest) says:

This is the Gospel of the Lord.

We answer:

PEOPLE: **Praise to you, Lord Jesus Christ.**

The homily

We sit down to listen to the priest. He invites and
encourages us to live according to the teachings
we have heard in the readings of the Word of God.

PROFESSION OF FAITH

The Creed is a prayer that goes back to the early days of the Church. In this prayer we express our faith. This means that we say what we believe about God and about the Church. Our parents and godparents professed this faith for us on the day of our Baptism.

PRIEST
& PEOPLE: **We believe in one God,**

> **the Father, the Almighty,**
> **maker of heaven and earth,**
> **of all that is, seen and unseen.**

We believe in one Lord,
> **Jesus Christ, the only Son of God,**
> **eternally begotten of the Father,**

God from God, Light from Light,
> **true God from true God,**

begotten, not made,
> **of one Being with the Father.**

Through him all things were made.

21

For us men and for our salvation
he came down from heaven: *All bow*
  by the power of the Holy Spirit
  he became incarnate
  from the Virgin Mary,
  and was made man.

For our sake he was crucified
under Pontius Pilate;
he suffered death and was buried.

On the third day
  he rose again
in accordance with the Scriptures;
  he ascended into heaven
  and is seated
at the right hand of the Father.

He will come again in glory
to judge the living and the dead,
and his kingdom will have no end.

We believe in the Holy Spirit,
  the Lord, the giver of life,
  who proceeds from the Father
  and the Son.

With the Father and the Son
he is worshipped and glorified.

He has spoken
through the Prophets.

We believe in one holy,
catholic and apostolic Church.

We acknowledge one baptism
for the forgiveness of sins.

We look for the resurrection
  of the dead,
  and the life
  of the world to come.
Amen.

The general intercessions
Prayer of the Faithful

Now we pray for the needs of the world, the Church, our country and our community.

To each short prayer we answer:

PEOPLE: **Lord, hear our prayer.**

    Or

    Lord, graciously hear us.

Give thanks

The Liturgy of the Eucharist

This is the second part of the Mass. The priest thanks God for all the wonderful things in the world and especially for the gift of his Son Jesus. In this part of the Mass the priest will recall the words and actions of Jesus at the Last Supper. The bread and wine will become Jesus' Body and Blood.

The presentation of the gifts

Bread and wine are brought to the altar.

Sometimes money and perhaps other things, for people in need, are also collected.

*Before placing the bread on the altar,
the priest says:*

PRIEST: Blessed are you, Lord, God of all
creation. Through your goodness we
have this bread to offer, which earth
has given and human hands have
made. It will become for us
the bread of life.

PEOPLE: **Blessed be God for ever.**

*Before placing the chalice (cup) of wine on the
altar, the priest says:*

PRIEST: Blessed are you, Lord, God of all
creation. Through your goodness we
have this wine to offer, fruit of the
vine and work of human hands.
It will become our spiritual drink.

PEOPLE: **Blessed be God for ever.**

Invitation to **prayer**

The priest invites us to pray to God to accept our gifts.

PRIEST: Pray, brethren, that my sacrifice
and yours may be acceptable to God,
the almighty Father.

PEOPLE: **May the Lord accept the sacrifice
at your hands for the praise
and glory of his name,
for our good,
and the good of all his Church.**

*The priest says a special prayer for today's Mass.
At the end, we all answer:*

PEOPLE: **Amen.**

We praise and thank God for all the beautiful things in our life

PRIEST: The Lord be with you.

PEOPLE: **And also with you.**

PRIEST: Lift up your hearts.

PEOPLE: **We lift them up to the Lord.**

PRIEST: Let us give thanks
to the Lord our God.

PEOPLE: **It is right to give him
thanks and praise.**

The priest now offers a prayer similar to this one:

PRIEST: Father, all powerful
and ever-living God,
we do well always and everywhere
to give you thanks.
In you we live and move
and have our being.

Each day you show us a Father's love;
your Holy Spirit, dwelling within us,
gives us on earth
the hope of unending joy.

Your gift of the Spirit,
who raised Jesus from the dead,
is the foretaste and promise
of the paschal feast of heaven.

With thankful praise,
in company with the angels,
we glorify the wonders
of your power:

At the end of this prayer we all sing:

**Holy, holy, holy Lord,
God of power and might,
heaven and earth
are full of your glory.**

**Hosanna in the highest.
Blessed is he who comes
in the name of the Lord.
Hosanna in the highest.**

We praise God
and ask him to accept our offering

Eucharistic Prayer III

The priest now offers this prayer or one similar to it:

PRIEST: Father, you are holy indeed,
        and all creation
           rightly gives you praise.

        All life, all holiness
           comes from you through your Son,
           Jesus Christ our Lord,
           by the working of the Holy Spirit.

        From age to age
           you gather a people to yourself,
           so that from east to west

a perfect offering may be made
to the glory of your name.

And so, Father,
we bring you these gifts.

We ask you to make them holy
by the power of your Spirit,
that they may become
the body and blood of your Son,
our Lord Jesus Christ,
at whose command
we celebrate this Eucharist.

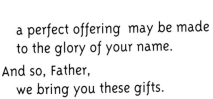

Our offering becomes the **body and blood** of Christ

PRIEST: On the night he was betrayed,
                 he took bread
                 and gave you thanks and praise.

           He broke the bread,
                 gave it to his disciples, and said:

**Take this,
     all of you,
          and eat it:**

this is my body

which will be
     given up for you.

32

When supper was ended,
he took the cup.

Again he gave you
    thanks and praise,
gave the cup to his disciples,
and said:

Take this,
  all of you,
    and drink from it:

this is the cup of my blood,

the blood of the new and
    everlasting covenant.
It will be shed for you
    and for all
      so that sins
        may be forgiven.

Do this **in memory** of me.

PRIEST: Let us proclaim the mystery of faith:

PEOPLE: **Christ has died,**
              Christ is risen,
                 Christ will come again.

Another acclamation may also be used.

We pray for one another

PRIEST: Father, calling to mind
              the death your Son endured
              for our salvation,
           his glorious resurrection and
              ascension into heaven,
           and ready to greet him
              when he comes again,
           we offer you in thanksgiving
              this holy and living sacrifice.

Look with favour
   on your Church's offering,
   and see the Victim
   whose death has reconciled us
   to yourself.
Grant that we, who are nourished
   by his body and blood,
may be filled with his Holy Spirit,
and become one body,
one spirit in Christ.

May he make us
   an everlasting gift to you
   and enable us to share
   in the inheritance of your saints,
with Mary, the virgin Mother of God;
with the apostles, martyrs,
(*the priest may name
   the saint of the day here*),
   and all your saints,
on whose constant intercession
   we rely for help.

We pray for **God's family**

PRIEST: Lord, may this sacrifice,
which has made our peace with you,
advance the peace
    and salvation of all the world.

Strengthen in faith and love
    your pilgrim Church on earth;
your servant, Pope
    (*the priest names our pope*),
our bishop
    (*the priest names our bishop*),
and all the bishops,
with the clergy and
    the entire people
    your Son has gained for you.

Father, hear the prayers
    of the family you have gathered
    here before you.

In mercy and love unite all your
   children wherever they may be.

Welcome into your kingdom
   our departed brothers and sisters,
and all who have left this world
   in your friendship.

We hope to enjoy for ever
   the vision of your glory,
through Christ our Lord,
   from whom all good things come.

*The priest raises the host and chalice to give glory
and praise to God through Jesus.*

PRIEST: **Through him,**
   with him,
      in him,
         in the unity
            of the Holy Spirit,
all glory and honour
   is yours,
      almighty Father,
         for ever and ever.

PEOPLE: **Amen.**

37

Share

Communion Rite

When we are invited to a party, we sing and we talk to one another. Then we eat what was prepared for us. God, our Father, has invited us to eat the bread of life, the Body and Blood of Jesus.

PRIEST: Let us pray with confidence
to the Father
in the words our Saviour gave us:

PEOPLE: **Our Father,
who art in heaven,
hallowed be thy name;
thy kingdom come;
thy will be done on earth,
as it is in heaven.**

**Give us this day our daily bread;
and forgive us our trespasses
as we forgive those
who trespass against us;
and lead us not into temptation,
but deliver us from evil.**

PRIEST: Deliver us, Lord, from every evil,
and grant us peace in our day.
In your mercy keep us free from sin
and protect us from all anxiety
as we wait in joyful hope
for the coming of our Saviour,
Jesus Christ.

PEOPLE: **For the kingdom,
the power and the glory
are yours,
now and for ever.**

The Sign of Peace

We pray for peace

PRIEST: Lord Jesus Christ,
you said to your apostles:
I leave you peace,
my peace I give you.

Look not on our sins,
but on the faith of your Church,
and grant us the peace
and unity of your kingdom
where you live for ever and ever.

PEOPLE: **Amen.**

PRIEST: The peace of the Lord
be with you always.

PEOPLE: **And also with you.**

The Priest may now say:

PRIEST: Let us offer each other
            the sign of peace.

*We give the peace of Jesus to each other with a
hand-shake, a hug or some other sign. In this way
we promise to love one another, to forgive one
another and to bring God's peace with us to our
home, our school and wherever we go.*

The breaking of the bread

The priest breaks the bread as Jesus did at the Last Supper. Meanwhile we sing or say:

PEOPLE: **Lamb of God,
you take away the sins
   of the world:
      have mercy on us.**

**Lamb of God,
you take away the sins
   of the world:
      have mercy on us.**

**Lamb of God,
you take away the sins
   of the world:
      grant us peace.**

Communion

The altar is like a table that has been set. The Supper of the Lord is ready and we are all invited. Jesus said: "I am the bread come down from heaven. If anyone eats this bread he will live for ever" (cf John 6:51). This special meal is a promise of the banquet that awaits us in heaven, where we will celebrate for ever.

PRIEST: This is the Lamb of God
who takes away
the sins of the world.

Happy are those who are called
to his supper.

PEOPLE: **Lord, I am not worthy
to receive you,
but only say the word
and I shall be healed.**

When we go up to receive communion, we express our faith again.

The priest or eucharistic minister offers me the host and says:

PRIEST: The body of Christ.

I ANSWER: **Amen.**

Then I receive the host on my tongue or in my hand.

At some Masses we can also receive the blood of Jesus Christ from the chalice. Jesus is there under the appearance of wine.

The priest or eucharistic minister offers me the chalice and says:

PRIEST: The blood of Christ.

I ANSWER: **Amen.**

Then I take a sip from the chalice.

We pray that **Jesus** within us will give us the **strength** to **love**

After communion we pray or sing a hymn of thanksgiving. We think about Jesus, who is in us, and we talk to him as our friend. We can tell him:

Lord Jesus, I thank you for the gift
    which you have given me.

Help me to be good, obedient and generous.

I pray for my parents,
    my brothers and sisters,
    and my friends.

I also pray for the Pope and for everybody
    who tries to do good for others.

I want everyone to know and love you.

I want to live in a way that pleases you.

Stay with me always, Lord Jesus.

I love you.

The priest says the prayer after communion. At the end of it, we all answer:

PEOPLE: **Amen.**

Tell everyone

Concluding Rite

The priest **blesses** us in God's name

PRIEST: The Lord be with you.

PEOPLE: **And also with you.**

PRIEST: May almighty God bless you,
the Father,
and the Son,
and the Holy Spirit.

PEOPLE: **Amen.**

PRIEST: The Mass is ended,
go in peace
to love and
serve the Lord.

PEOPLE: **Thanks be to God.**

After a party, before leaving, we say thank you to whoever has invited us. In the same way at the end of our celebration we may say thank you to God with a song. Then we go out to bring to others the love that we have received from God.

Going to meet Jesus

Jesus is present

Some of the hosts that were consecrated at Mass and left over are kept in the tabernacle to be taken to the sick and also to be adored by us. A small light is always burning to remind us that the Eucharist is Jesus, really and truly alive and present.

During the day try to visit Jesus. You can talk to him about the things that are important to you. Then listen in silence. Jesus will speak in your heart. You might use these words to pray to Jesus:

Jesus, I believe that you are here,
    that you watch over me
    and listen to my prayers.
You are my very best friend.
You are always close to me,
    and to everyone who wants to love
    and obey you.
But you are also close to those
    who want to live without you.
You love them too.
And you want us to pray for them.

Even though I cannot see you,
        I believe that you are with me.
Help me to love everyone I meet
        and notice people who need help.
I pray for all who are suffering.
I pray for all who are sick and have problems.
I thank you for everything you have given me.
Help me to share with others, Jesus.
Amen.

*It is an important duty to take part in the
celebration of Mass every Sunday. God our
Father asks us to love him and to live as
his friends at home, at school and at play.*

*It is not always easy to live in a way that pleases
God. And so we need to ask God's forgiveness for
our sins and to receive communion often. This is
the only way we can be strong enough to live the
most important commandment Jesus gave us:
"Love one another as I have loved you".
(cf John 13:34)*

The Sacrament of Reconciliation

There are many ways in which we admit that we have done wrong and ask forgiveness of God and of others. But the greatest way that brings us the forgiveness of God and others is the sacrament of reconciliation.

Celebrate the sacrament of reconciliation by first of all recognising the great love that God has for you. Thank him for the gift of life, for the love of your parents, relatives and friends. You might want to pray using these words:

Your love is boundless, Lord

I praise you, Lord,
> with everything that I am
> and everything that I do.
I praise your holy name.
I remember all the
wonderful things
you do for me.

You are so merciful and kind.
When I do something wrong,
    you do not get angry with me.
You forgive me.
You help me to do better next time.

Your kindness is so great
    to those who love you, Lord.
It is as great as the space
    that separates the earth
    from the heavens.
Let everything he has created
    praise the Lord.
I praise you, Lord.

Based on Psalm 103

My examination of conscience

Now think about your life. See how you have obeyed the Ten Commandments, the laws that God gave to Moses. If you look in your Bible you will find these laws in Exodus 20:2-17 and Deuteronomy 5:6-21. Jesus summed up the Ten Commandments in his law of love: "Love one another as I have loved you" in John's Gospel: 15:12.

1. I am the Lord your God: you shall not have strange gods before me.

Each morning and evening do I remember to pray to God who loves me? Do I thank him for all the good things he has done for me?

2. You shall not take the name of the Lord, your God, in vain.

Have I used God's name or the name of Jesus in the wrong way, in joking around or when I was angry?

3. Remember to keep holy the Lord's day.

Have I gone to Mass on Sundays (or Saturday evenings) each week? Do I go to all my catechism classes? Do I help others to celebrate at Mass by smiling and being happy?

4. Honour your father and your mother.

Do I sometime talk back to my parents? Have I done what they told me to do? Do I listen to their advice? Do I help out around the house?

5. You shall not kill.

Have I been angry with others? Have I wanted to hurt them in some way? Have I fought with my brothers and sisters? Have I hurt anybody on purpose?

6. You shall not commit adultery.

Do I thank the Lord for the gift of my body and for all the many things I can do with it, especially showing care and love for others? Do I treat my body and everyone else's body with respect and care? Do I look only at pictures and watch tv shows and videos that are good?

7. You shall not steal.

Have I taken anything that did not belong to me? Have I returned things which I borrowed? Do I show respect and care for the environment around me?

8. You shall not bear false witness.

Do I always tell the truth, even when it may be hard? When I have done something wrong, do I admit it? Have I lied about others?

 9. You shall not desire
your neighbour's wife.

Am I jealous when someone I like likes somebody else? Am I envious of the friends of others?

10. You shall not desire
your neighbour's goods.

Do I wish I had what belongs to someone else? Am I happy to see others happy? Do I mind helping people who are poor?

*You might like to say this prayer based
on the Canticle of Azariah from the Book
of Daniel in your Bible: Daniel 3:26-45.*

Accept us, **Lord**

We praise you, Lord.
You are the God of our Fathers.
You, more than anyone else,
are worthy to be praised and glorified forever.
We admit that we have done things
     that were wrong.
We have sinned against you
     and have not loved you as we should.
We have not always obeyed
     the commandments which you gave us
     for our own good.
Please be merciful to us, Lord.
We promise to do better
     and to follow you with all our heart.
We do not want to offend you again.
We want to be close to you.
Treat us with kindness and compassion.
Save us with your wonderful power, Lord.
Give glory to your name.

My confession

The priest represents Jesus and the Church. When you go to confess your sins he will welcome you and listen to you as a good father.

PRIEST: In the name of the Father
          and of the Son and of the Holy Spirit.

I ANSWER: **Amen.**

PRIEST: May the grace of the Holy Spirit
              fill your heart with light,
          that you may confess
              your sins with loving trust
              and come to know
              that God is merciful.

The priest may use different words to greet you. Next, the priest may read from the Bible about how good God is and how ready he is to forgive.

Tell the priest your sins as honestly as you can. Accept the prayers or good deeds that he gives you as a penance. This shows that you want to live a new life. The priest will then ask you to tell God you are sorry for your sins.

Lord, I am **sorry!**

You can use these words or others like them:

My God, because you are so good,
I am very sorry that I have sinned against you.
With the help of your grace,
I will try not to sin again.
Amen.

Or:

Lord Jesus, Son of God,
    I am really sorry
    for anything wrong I have done.
Please forgive me.

After you say your prayer of sorrow, the priest will pray these words in the name of Jesus:

PRIEST: God, the Father of mercies,
               through the death
               and resurrection of his Son
               has reconciled the world
               to himself
               and sent the Holy Spirit among us
               for the forgiveness of sins.

               Through the ministry of the Church
               may God give you pardon
               and peace,
               and I absolve you from your sins
               in the name of the Father,
               and of the Son,
               and of the Holy Spirit.

I ANSWER: **Amen**

PRIEST: Give thanks to the Lord for he is good.

I ANSWER: **His mercy endures for ever.**

PRIEST: The Lord has freed you from your sins.

               Go in peace.

61

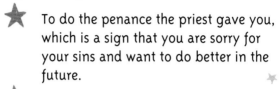

After confession **remember...**

★ To do the penance the priest gave you, which is a sign that you are sorry for your sins and want to do better in the future.

★ There is joy in heaven when one sinner on earth is sorry.

★ There is joy when Christians celebrate God's forgiveness.

★ There is joy when we, who have known God's goodness, take his peace out to the whole world.

Take some time to thank God and ask him to help you keep your promises to be better. You might like to use this prayer or make one in your own words:

I thank you, Lord, for having forgiven me

I praise you Lord.
With all the love that is in me
I praise your holy name.
You forgive all my sins, Lord,
    and you heal all my weakness.
You bless me with love
    and compassion.
You make me feel strong
    and happy,
        just like an eagle flying
        high in the sky.
You do not treat me
    according to the mistakes
    I have made.
You do not repay me for my sins.
Your love for me, Lord, will last for ever.

Based on Psalm 103